JESUS SAID

"I AM"

An Artistic Exploration
of the Seven "I AM's"
of Jesus

by Rachael Lofgren
Illustrated by Patti Lofgren

SINGING
SPARROW
PRESS

BEMIDJI, MINNESOTA

Scripture copyright info:

All Scripture quotations, unless otherwise indicated, are taken from the Holy Bible, New International Version®, NIV®. Copyright © 1973, 1978, 1984, 2011 by Biblica, Inc.® Used by permission of Zondervan. All rights reserved worldwide. www.zondervan.com. The "NIV" and "New International Version" are trademarks registered in the United States Patent and Trademark Office by Biblica, Inc.®

Scripture quotations marked NLT are taken from the Holy Bible, New Living Translation. Copyright © 1996, 2004, 2015 by Tyndale House Foundation. Used by permission of Tyndale House Publishers, Carol Stream, Illinois 60188. All rights reserved.

Scripture quotations marked KJV are taken from the King James Version. Public domain.

Artwork reference photos:

Special thanks to those who graciously shared artist reference photos,
and to those whose work was found in the Commons and used for that purpose.

Works from the Creative Commons used as reference:
39: AI generated Woman Gate, Dexmac via Pixabay

Licensed works used for reference with purchase and/or permissions:
18: Communion Bread & Wine, Romolo Tavani
27: Jesus Writing in the Sand, R Gino Santa Maria
43: Nazareth Shepherd, Nopow
47: Shepherd Holding Lamb, Milena Magazin

Jesus Said "I AM"

Dedication

With love for I AM, who gives us our identity as children of God.

In you, we live, move, and have our being.
In your light, we see the light.
And in your love, we find home.
We adore you!

Table of Contents

How to Read This Book

This book consists of an intro on God's name as "I AM," followed by seven sets of four meditations—one set for each of Jesus's seven I AM's, as revealed in the gospels.

The arrangement of the readings in each set of meditations represents and celebrates Triune God's story as I AM revealed in Father, Son, and Holy Spirit, who bears witness to the world through his body, the church.

God, whose name is I AM, introduced himself with specific characteristics (I AM the Bread of Life, etc.). I AM's character is evident in the story of God and his people in the Old or First Covenant. Jesus revealed I AM as a personal and redeeming God more fully in the gospels, completing the work of redemption at the cross. By the power of his Holy Spirit, this revelation transforms the lives of redeemed believers in the body of Christ, equipping them to live as God's children in the world. Filled with the counsel and comfort of the Holy Spirit, who is the presence of God in the world, we abide in I AM, whom we love and follow, participating in his work in the world and bearing witness to the gospel, with the anticipation that Jesus is returning soon.

I AM, Redeemer God, made known through the revelation of his Son Jesus, reflected by the power of his Holy Spirit in his people— the body of Christ.

The first meditation of each set is an introduction in poetry of a specific I AM characteristic of the name and nature of God.

The second meditation is on how Redeemer God is displayed in each of the seven I AM characteristics in the Old Testament.

The third meditation highlights the Revelation of God through Jesus as I AM in the gospels.

The fourth meditation is on the Reflection of I AM's character in the lives of Jesus' transformed followers by the power of his Holy Spirit.

Background

"I AM WHO I AM"

Moses said to God, "Suppose I go to the Israelites and say to them, 'The God of your fathers has sent me to you,' and they ask me, **'What is his name?' Then what shall I tell them?"**

God said to Moses, "I am who I am. *This is what you are to say to the Israelites: 'I am has sent me to you. " God also said to Moses, "Say to the Israelites, 'The* LORD, *the God of your fathers—the God of Abraham, the God of Isaac and the God of Jacob—has sent me to you.' This is my name forever, the name you shall call me from generation to generation."* (Ex. 3:13-15 NIV)

Then the LORD *came down in the cloud and stood there with him and proclaimed his name, the* LORD. *And he passed in front of Moses, proclaiming, "The* LORD, *the* LORD, *the compassionate and gracious God, slow to anger, abounding in love and faithfulness, maintaining love to thousands, and forgiving wickedness, rebellion and sin. Yet he does not leave the guilty unpunished; he punishes the children and their children for the sin of the parents to the third and fourth generation."*

Moses bowed to the ground at once and worshiped. (Ex. 34:5-8 NIV)

Jesus said I AM:

The Bread of Life

The Light of the World

The Door to the Sheepfold

The Good Shepherd

The Resurrection and the Life

The Way, Truth, and Life

The True Vine

Coming Soon

Introduction

COVENANT WITH "I AM"

Etched in stone, the words "*No other gods*" are a command and an invitation to the covenant community of Israel (Ex. 20:3, NLT). God alone has brought them out of hundreds of years of slavery in a showdown between the gods of Egypt and the living God.

Taking them into the wilderness, with the shepherd warrior Moses in the lead and setting their feet on the path to promise, God brings them to the Mountain of Sinai. Now, he speaks again, inviting them into vows of Covenant with himself. The I AM who introduced himself at the flaming bush to Moses reiterates his name and character: "*I AM the Lord your God who rescued you...*" (Ex 20:2).

The I AM who is compassionate, merciful, loving, and faithful offers himself to the people he has named his own. "I AM ready to lavish my faithful and loyal love on you to a thousand generations" he declares. "I will forgive your sins; I AM slow to anger and gracious."

But they are afraid of his jealous, exclusive offer. They have long been used to four hundred years of man's violent oppression and God's seeming silence. They are not used to his voice and its power. Nor are they used to his commanding and loving presence.

They draw back, fearing for their lives. Moses, who has walked in the presence of God, reassures them that the fear of God is given to keep them from sin, not to keep them from God. This powerful love longs to restore them to flourish in his presence. He is not a slave master but a passionate bridegroom, restoring his people to their rightful place in relationship to him.

"Build an altar...I will come to you and bless you..." he instructs Moses.

And over and over again, since he made man in his image, the I AM has been speaking the same message, drawing and pursuing his people in love, longing to bless them with restoration to himself and to home.

In Jesus, I AM finishes this work once and for all at the cross. The Godman ushers in the kingdom of faithful justice and merciful love as a new covenant, renewing his vows of faithfulness and compassion to his people. Only his sacrifice will be enough to enact permanent redemption. So, in his ultimate revelation of redemptive and faithful love, he pours out his life to save his people from the sin and shame that separates them from flourishing life at home in his presence. He finishes what he started by conquering death in his resurrection and inviting his people into eternal life through believing in his name.

Today, we, his people, live in the kingdom of heaven coming, and the hope of the final coming of I AM to set things eternally right in his loyal faithfulness to his people of the New Covenant, the Church. While we wait, we live on a mission to be compassionate, gracious, and faithful representatives of the good I AM in the world. We seek to establish and facilitate people's flourishing through living by God's justice and mercy. And through his Spirit, he is with us always to the end of the age. The Way, the Truth, and the Life has gone to prepare a place for us. And soon, we will be home with him forever.

I AM

the Bread of Life

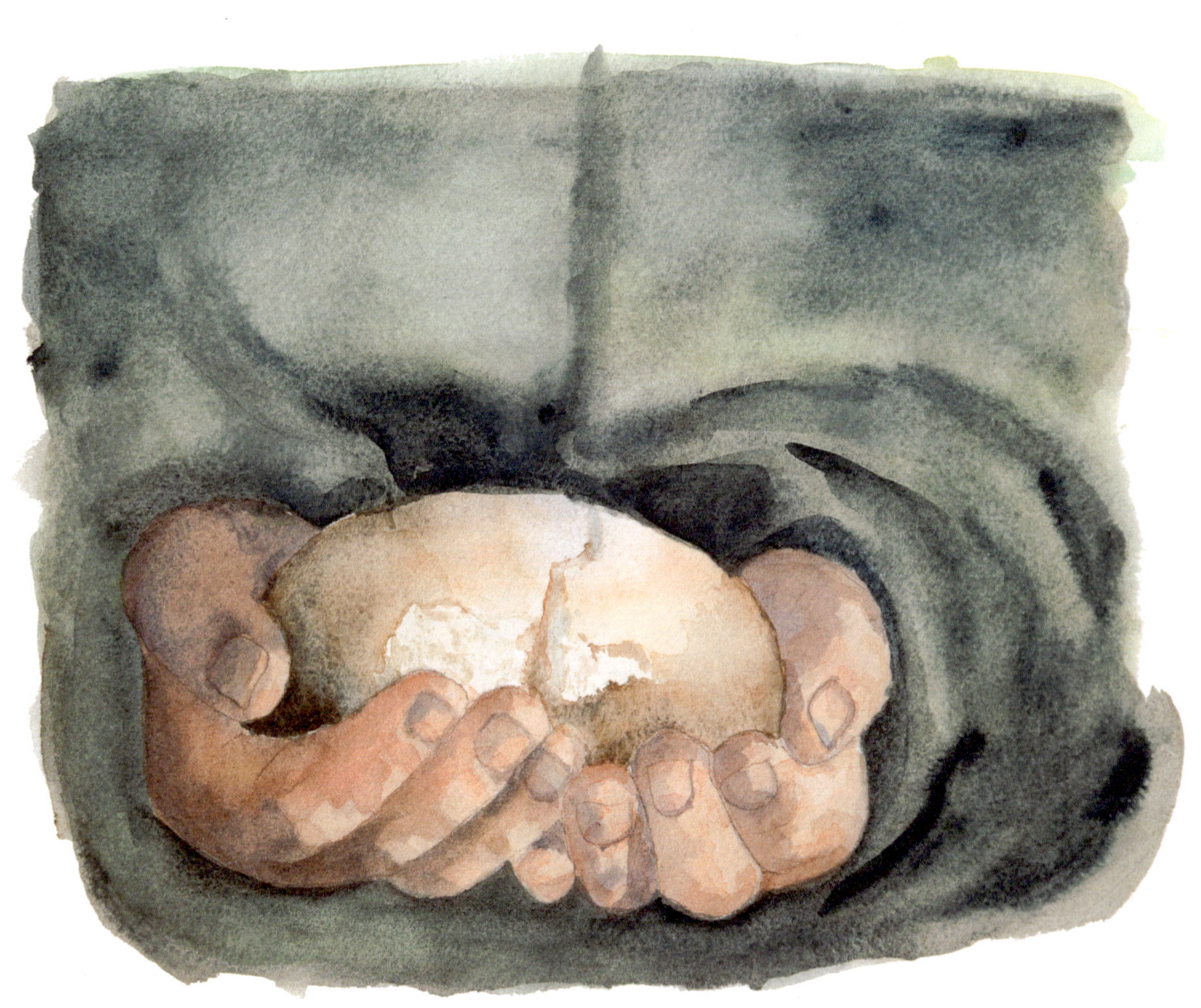

Broken and Given

Designed with desire
Born crying – knowing need
Humanity hungers for sustaining
To feed the life we have been given

In the wilderness – Manna
Daily bread – hunger filled
Spiritual souls craving something
The longing for the Bread of Life

Feeding Five-Thousand
"Give us more bread"
This bread is my body broken
Eat my flesh – this is a mystery

Bread Broken and given
Jesus - Sustainer of all things
Seed of wheat, dying and buried
Grows into a harvest of abundant life

Communion of his body
In remembrance – break bread
Live resurrection forever life in me
Be broken to feed the world with love

Bread from Heaven

EXODUS SIXTEEN (NIV)

"What is it?" Talia asks her neighbor.

"I don't know." Dinah shrugs. "It looks like frost."

"But the sun has already burned the dew away, so it can't be frost." Sarah joins them from the doorway of her tent, looking at the thin white flakes scattered across the desert sand.

"What is it?" isn't a new question for the Israelites. On their strange journey through the wilderness, every day brings surprises. They are still less than hungry after the quail appeared from nowhere last night. The smell of cooked poultry and smoke from thousands of cooking fires still lingers heavy in the air. Speaking of strange, it's only been six weeks since they walked through the Red Sea on dry ground.

Moses solves the morning mystery of the little white flakes for them.

> *It is the bread the Lord has given you to eat. This is what the Lord has commanded: "Everyone is to gather as much as they need. Take an omer for each person you have in your tent." (Ex 16:16, NIV)*

"Tastes like wafers made with honey." Talia decides as she lets the white substance melt on her tongue. They choose to call the bread "manna" meaning "What is it?

The rejoicing about bread from heaven is a quick turn from yesterday's heaviness. The beginning of the manna story falls right in the middle of a communal grumbling party. The Israelites, fresh out of slavery, wandering in the Desert of Sin,

freak out about the future. Farming isn't in the cards here. And in Egypt, they never had to worry about food. They might be beaten to death on any given day. But at least they had food to eat! The uncertainty of freedom feels scarier to them than the certainty of slavery or even death.

> *If only we had died by the Lord's hand in Egypt! There we sat around pots of meat and ate all the food we wanted, but you have brought us out into this desert to starve this entire assembly to death. (16:3)*

Weary, disgruntled thousands throw their accusations at Moses and Aaron. In the middle of their fearful whining, God invites them to faith. To them, that faith looks like a risk. How do they know that God will be faithful to them? God meets them with a promise.

In this desolate, barren landscape where the earth cracks with thirst and nothing grows green, God says,

> *I will rain down bread from heaven for you. The people are to go out each day and gather enough for that day. In this way, I will test them and see whether they will follow my instructions. On the sixth day, they are to prepare what they bring in, and that is to be twice as much as they gather on the other days...I have heard the grumbling of the Israelites. Tell them, "At twilight, you will eat meat, and in the morning, you will be filled with bread. Then you will know that I am the LORD your God." (16:4-5, 12)*

He moves toward them compassionately, even as he holds them accountable to faith. They had seen the character of God in deliverance, but they have not yet come to depend on him in a trusting relationship, confident in his provision of daily sustenance. Slavery has taught them to be fearful. Now God has to retrain them to trust, by choice, in his goodness.

This exact pattern will continue with the new mercy of bread every morning for as long as the wilderness wanderings last. Not one day, no matter how the people fail him, will God fail to provide for his people the sustenance they need to live. He sends a fresh supply daily with a double portion for the Sabbath. They eat this Manna for forty years until they enter the promised land. This is the faithful provision of God.

Bread of Life

JOHN SIX (NIV)

The crowds have been searching for Jesus since the big miracle yesterday. Feeding five thousand people with five loaves of bread doesn't just happen every day. Imagine it! One loaf of bread per a thousand people. This man is sure to be a prophet from God.

When the crowd can't find him, they get into boats and cross the lake. He must be on the other side. Sure enough. That's where they find him, teaching in a Synagogue in Capernaum.

When they ask him where he's been, Jesus responds. "You aren't looking for me because of the miracle. You are looking for me because of the bread you ate to fill your hunger. Don't work for food that spoils. Look to me for food that endures to eternal life that I can give you. Believing in me is the work that God invites you to do."

They bring up the bread from heaven, then. Asking what signs he'll do for them to prove himself. "Our fathers ate the manna in the wilderness. What will you do?"

He enlightens them. It's not about the manna. It's about the bread of God that comes down from heaven and gives life to the world. "I AM the Bread of Life! No one who comes to me will be hungry anymore. Anyone who believes in me has eternal life as my Father wills."

He speaks to their true hunger. But they can't hear him. They argue instead because he says he's come down from heaven. "Isn't he just that carpenter's son?" They don't have room in their hearts or minds for the deeper truth he is revealing. Yet he persists in his declaration. Aching for them to see. Aching to receive them and fill their hunger with himself.

No one can come to me unless the Father who sent me draws them, and I will raise them up at the last day. It is written in the Prophets: 'They will all be taught by God.' Everyone who has heard the Father and learned from him comes to me. No one has seen the Father except the one who is from God; only he has seen the Father. Very truly, I tell you, the one who believes has eternal life. I AM the bread of life. Your ancestors ate the manna in the wilderness, yet they died. But here is the bread that comes down from heaven, which anyone may eat and not die. I AM the living bread that came down from heaven. Whoever eats this bread will live forever. This bread is my flesh, which I will give for the life of the world. (Jn 6:45-51, NIV)

This is our Jesus, who willingly gave his body to be broken in the greatest sacrifice of all time to bring us the bread of salvation. Jesus, born in the house of bread, filling God's House with the nourishment of eternal life. Jesus, revealing the faithful character of God as the bread of life.

He, the source of all life, was broken as a grain of wheat, falling into the ground to die, springing up into the resurrection of eternal life. Behold the broken bread given for the life of the whole world.

Bread of Communion

I recently sat with a friend sharing the grief of brokenness in a deeply valued relationship. As we cried, prayed, and reached for hope, I felt the Spirit of God ministering in our midst. As we talked, we acknowledged that the way God held us in our brokenness gave us what was needed to comfort others in their pain. Seeing my friend to the door to say goodbye late that evening, I felt Jesus whisper to my heart, "This is my body broken for you." At that moment, I glimpsed the beauty of a lived communion. We, the body of Christ to one another, share in the fellowship of his suffering and the hope of his comfort through the Comforter, his Spirit in us and through us.

It reminds me of a communion many years ago while traveling abroad. I was attending a prayer conference in Asia. When the time came to share the sacrament of communion, I wanted to participate in this meaningful remembrance with the several hundred brothers and sisters gathered from around the world. But at that time, I had developed allergies to both elements and could not physically partake. As I stood next to Elizabeth, my new friend from India, whom I'd just met at the dinner table a short time before, I knew what I would do. I drummed up my courage and whispered my predicament to her.

"Will you drink my juice and eat my bread?" I asked. "I want to partake, but I have allergies."

"I'd be so happy to," she responded without hesitation.

When the elements were passed, I took my portion. I quietly passed them to Elizabeth, and she took them along with her own while my heart felt the weight and joy of remembering the sacrifice of Jesus, along with the rest of the congregation. In those moments, I was reminded again of the beauty of the body of Christ in communion. To me, the symbolism of that shared communion was more potent than the taste of any physical reminder I could have partaken in. It was a tangible representation of "This is my body that holds you in your brokenness as you remember together. This is the true communion of the people of God as you live in communities of love."

And always, I remember, the last supper. That first communion, before the cross. When he took the bread in his hands, hands that would soon feel the cold anguish of nails and splintered wood, he broke it. Giving the fragrant pieces to his beloved followers to eat, he told them, *This is my body, given for you; do this in remembrance of me*" (Lk 22:19b NIV).

After supper, Jesus washed his follower's feet. He called them to the humble service of love. To go lower. To see each other and care for one another. To lay down their lives. "By this, all the world will know they are my followers if they love one another." This is the communion of saints. This love—only nourished by remembering the greatest Love of all. And as we remember Jesus, the Bread of Life, broken for us, we find the shared bread of communion in the community of saints—the broken body of Christ.

I AM

the Light of the World

Illuminate

Light of light in all your glory
Word that spoke the sun and moon
Stars called forth in singing beauty
All the universe attuned

In your light we see Illumined
Fount of life – and crystal sea
Future of a heavenly story
Reflected in the mystery

Of an earthly image mirroring
God in man and man in Christ
Light in earthen vessels dwelling
This the power of sacrifice

Darkened hour, the cross, the dying
Then the triumph ore' the tomb
New life born in resurrection
Spirit filling the upper room

This the people of a Savior
Let your light, so shine he said
God commanded out of darkness
Light that leads the way ahead

In our hearts this light now living
Illuminates the knowledge given
God's eternal glorious presence
In the face of Jesus risen!

Let There Be Light

There is darkness, and there is Triune God. Then the Spirit of God moves and speaks. The Word of God says, *"Let there be light!"* (Gen 1:3, NLT).

And there is LIGHT! Beautiful golden white brightness in reflecting, refracting illumination. It bursts into the darkness of the cosmos, dispelling the shadows of nothingness. The light warms and prepares the space where unformed earth, held in the womb of God's desire, waits to transform into a haven of beauty and goodness. Revealing the creative canvas on which God will masterfully design the rest of the world.

Warmth! Color! Vibrant energy pulses everywhere. Light will fuel reproduction and growth and energize the bursting forth of plant and animal life. Light will be the guiding source for perception and interaction for all living organisms' seeing, feeling, and growth. Light will be essential to the survival and thriving it will nurture in all living things.

God sees the light. And he calls it good. It reflects his nature. His goodness. His Name. In his light, all living things will see light and be invited to drink from his fountain of life.

He divides the light from darkness and calls the light day, which will be ruled by the closest star to earth: the sun. The night, too, will have its lights, the Moon and stars, called forth by name, singing their Creator's praise and filling the universe with awe. The heavens declare his glory, morning and evening, in spectacular sunrises and sunsets. Light reflects his faithfulness, guiding the turning of seasons and marking the passing of time. Light will fill the earth with his beauty and goodness for thousands of years.

Light sets the atmosphere for displaying glory. It reveals the character of the Life-giver from whom all goodness comes. Light reflects the presence of God and a day coming eternally where there will be no night. He will be the light of that Heavenly City. His people will walk in the glorious light of his presence forever, knowing fully as they are known.

Light of the World

The people have been accusing him of demon possession. Even his own brothers doubt his identity. Still, Jesus seems mostly unphased. He knows who he is. He goes about his Father's will with calm determination.

Always trying to trick him, the religious leaders bring a woman caught in adultery to him. He knows they want to accuse him. They are fully engaged in a fight with him over his identity and the certainty of his testimony. Still, he shames them into silence with a single wise sentence. He ends the conversation with only the woman and himself left in that dusty circle. *"Neither do I condemn you"* (Jn 8:11, NIV).

The next time he speaks, he is in the temple courts. Here he declares another beautiful aspect of his character. *"I AM the light of the world. Whoever follows me will never walk in darkness, but will have the light of life"* (Jn 8:12).

The religious leaders are angry. The argument lasts a heated while and ends with them picking up rocks to bash Jesus' head in. Jesus slips away from them. They will see the light when he is lifted up. He has told them this. But they do not want to see. They will be the instigators of his death.

John, his beloved disciple, will later write his biography in the gospel of John, using Jesus' vivid words about light to introduce his beloved Messiah. He starts at the beginning of time when the character of God was declared through the creation of life and light.

In the beginning was the Word, and the Word was with God, and the Word was God. He was with God in the beginning. Through him, all things were made; without him, nothing was made that has been made. In him was life, and that life was the light of all mankind. The light shines in the darkness, and the darkness has not overcome it. The true light that gives light to everyone was coming into the world. He was in the world, and though the world was made through him, the world did not recognize him. He came to that which was his own, but his own did not receive him. Yet to all who did receive him, to those who believed in his name, he gave the right to become children of God The Word became flesh and made his dwelling among us. We have seen his glory, the glory of the one and only Son, who came from the Father, full of grace and truth. (Jn 1:1-5, 9-12, 14)

Let Your Light Shine

The sun has set over the western horizon. Lights begin to twinkle on one by one in the streets of our village as dusk fades to twilight. The old stone castle on the hill shines out brightly in the deepening darkness of the night. Its golden yellow radiance is distinct from all the lesser lights of homes, street lamps, and shop windows sprawled below it.

When I see that ancient castle lit up in the dark, I think of Jesus' words to his followers. In his sermon on another mountain a few countries over from where I live and work, he speaks about light and villages and hills just like this one.

> *You are the light of the world. A town built on a hill cannot be hidden. Neither do people light a lamp and put it under a bowl. Instead, they put it on its stand, and it gives light to everyone in the house. In the same way, let your light shine before others, that they may see your good deeds and glorify your Father in heaven.* (Matt 5:14-16, NIV)

I have just returned from supper with a friend. She is a middle-aged professional with a bright mind and a friendly smile. But under the surface, she is reeling from her world, torn apart by domestic abuse. She has violated cultural shame and honor norms, and her father is enraged. She has shown me the bruises. Her words have shown me her soul. The darkness of pain seeps into all of her words as we finish supper and coffee. And it is there in the mix of pain and darkness that light breaks through.

She wants to hear the story of Jesus. She listens. She reaches for the beauty, albeit blindly. And like the woman in the dust of another time caught in vulnerable shame, she hears that he does not condemn her but invites her into his nearness. She is comforted by prayer for her healing and her future.

On the way to the car, she clings to my arm. "You are so calm. I need your strength." She leans into me, broken by the pain. Reaching for the light. For months to come, I will meet with my friend for coffee, sometimes on her balcony, sometimes in the village's cobbled square. And often, I pray for her that the goodness of my Father will draw her to glorify him.

This is why we are here. As Jesus' followers, we long in our actions and words to introduce our neighbors and friends to the beauty of the Messiah and the goodness of his message.

But we are aware that we cannot do this alone. In our work and relationships, we are consistently reminded that this treasure of light through Christ has been placed in earthen vessels. Our own earthiness and limits, and failures keep us humbly and sometimes desperately asking for his light to fill us. And in answer, this goodness of God, light shining out of darkness, is empowered by God's Spirit when we say yes to him.

We see it in the shy smiles of a teenager understanding the power of the cross for the first time and in the lisping prayers of a child as he copies

our words to Isa the Messiah with shining eyes. The light is breaking into the darkness.

In forgiveness after failure, hope after tragedy, and the worship of many nationalities, all in unity in our international community, we cultivate this beauty. And in shared meals and laughter, we see the light in one another and remember our calling again. We are the light of the world. We live in the beauty and goodness of the kingdom of heaven coming and the kingdom yet to come. Our greatest joy is to glorify our Father in heaven, shining like stars in a dark world, carrying his light in our small human frames with love.

I AM

the Door

The Open Door to Home

I AM the Gate
The Open Door to home
The Way to God
And I say come

Come follow me
Come here and find your rest
Come be my sheep
Words you can trust.

Banished by Mercy

GENESIS THREE

It's a wretched scene after so much beauty. The banishment of our first parents from the perfect garden. The ground is cursed. Reproduction is cursed. Their work is cursed. All of creation is under the blight of sin and separation. A shadow cast over the beauty of that easy intimate walking and working with God in a good and perfect world. All because of a single choice.

The first rendition of ashes to ashes and dust to dust has been spoken. Death has entered the scene. "You were taken from the dust, and you shall be returned to dust." God tells them. He has clothed their naked bodies with skins, but he has not yet made the way to remove the sense of shame from their souls. The shadows of sorrow are immense for the created man and the good God who made him. Separation is not his design.

But God is not just concerned about the temporary demise of his creation. The Tree of Life stands in the garden. Another temptation for man is to take and eat that which is forbidden. If the man eats it, he will live forever. Living under the curse eternally is not part of God's good plan. This is why he banishes Adam and Eve. He drives out his friends, created in his image, casting them from Eden for their own protection. "You must work the ground from which you have been taken." Words hard with severe mercy.

He sets a Cherubim on the east side of Eden. The flaming sword flashes back and forth like a warning beacon. Do not enter here. The Tree of Life is under guard. This, too, is for the man's protection and redemption. Because God has a plan. A way to form a passageway back to fellowship with God—the door to restored connection and communion with their Creator.

For centuries this story will be woven into the meaning of the story of God's people. It will be woven into the promises of the covenant, the shadows of the Tabernacle, the foretelling of the prophesies, and the prayers of the Psalms. God will make a way back for his people. He will not leave them separated forever. But for now, the door is closed. The gate shut to Eden. The unbroken fellowship marred by sin's curse. Only God's Son himself can reverse it. Only he can reveal the doorway back to the safe pasture of redemption.

The Gate to Life

JOHN NINE (NIV)

"I can see! I can see!" the wonder of a world in full color is still transformatively fresh for the man born blind. But his rejoicing is clouded by the hostile response of his community leaders. Their anger baffles him. Isn't a miracle a good thing?

"I am sure this man is from God, or he couldn't do this healing work." He protests.

"You're a born sinner." His local synagogue leaders throw him out. "How dare you lecture us!"

Jesus meets him in this moment of rejection. Looking into this man's healed physical eyes, Jesus seeks to open his spiritual ones by revealing his identity. "Do you place belief in the Son of Man?"

"Who is he?"

"You've seen him, and actually, he's speaking to you right now." I can hear the smile in Jesus' voice.

The man declares his devotion. "Of course, I believe!" And he worships.

He heals a blind man, and he declares himself to be the way to God. The Pharisees cannot bear the influence and certainty of this Rabbi. It drives them mad. So they keep hounding Jesus. They won't let up till they are rid of him.

Jesus tells them they are spiritually blind, but their actual sin lies in their denial of their blindness. Their hostile and religious response is to hate him all the more. In the ongoing heated conversation, Jesus addresses their prideful leadership and parallels it with his selfless Shepherding.

Very truly, I tell you, I AM the gate for the sheep. All who have come before me are thieves and robbers, but the sheep have not listened to them. I AM the gate; whoever enters through me will be saved. They will come in and go out and find pasture. The thief comes only to steal and kill and destroy; I have come that they may have life and have it to the full. (John 10:7b-10, NIV)

Don't you see that the religious spirit of the law only kills, steals, and destroys? Don't you know that I AM the fulfillment of all your prophesies? I AM the leader who will take you into life. I AM the shepherd with the divine authority to open the passageway to God. I AM the One who can protect you and give you good pasture and abundant eternal life. I AM the only way to salvation.

But they don't see. They don't see that the redemption promised in the garden of the way back to God is fulfilled in their presence. They do not hear the joy that the long-awaited Messiah has arrived. They do not recognize that Jesus is the only way back to God. Instead, they press into their self-reliance, religious works, and rigorous control and power systems.

They have tried to get rid of him many times, yet he dodges them every time. They call him demon-possessed, which seems to be their favorite curse to fling at him besides "blasphemer." Then, when they can't silence him or back him down, they pick up stones to kill him.

Yet, the blind man who receives the I AM by faith has entered a new way of life filled with hope and wonder. He has seen the Messiah with his own eyes and been transformed.

At the cross, Jesus will open that door to life forever. The way will be made. "I AM the gate. I AM the door. I AM the only way to God. I AM the salvation you seek." The curtain of separation will be torn in two, and the communion in the garden will be restored in eternal life.

Open the Door!

The white rock banks stretch away above us, tier on tier. Bowl after bowl of blue hot springs dimples the pure white rock, flowing one into another. Dipping my toes in the silky hot water, I grin. Visiting these calcium-rich thermal pools in Pammukale is our first stop of the day. My group and I agree there is a reason this is the top tourist attraction in the country. The natural surroundings are surreal, with stunning white and blue sprawling over the hillside. The "Cotton Castle" of Türkiye is an incredible natural wonder.

Ten kilometers south of Pammukale are the ancient ruins of the famed "lukewarm" church of Laodicea. We wander the ruins and wonder about this church that receives such a stiff warning in Revelation. We know their legacy doesn't end with lukewarmness from the geological ruins unearthed in recent years. But at the time they receive the warning, they are clearly a grief to the heart of the Savior they profess to follow.

The temptation to partake in the wealth and prestige of the Roman Empire has proven too much for this affluent church. They are self-sufficient and worldly. Partaking in this power and wealth at the cost of compromise, they have avoided persecution but have left the Christ they claim to follow outside the closed door. The gate of salvation they entered through has lost its focus in their lives. They do not feel they need a Savior. They've got this on their own.

Jesus calls them to account. He reminds them of the neighboring town of Colosse with clear cold water. It's not cold by the time it reaches the town of Laodicea, though. Then there are the hot springs of Hierapolis down the road. This water has powerful healing properties in its warmth. But the water loses its heat by the time it reaches their town. Laodicea is notorious for its water troubles. Lukewarm water is a metaphor this church understands, despite their posh resources in other arenas. Jesus says he's getting ready to vomit them out of his mouth in disgust if they don't recognize their need for him because this lukewarm blindness and spiritual poverty has led to their uselessness in their kingdom calling.

> You say, "I am rich; I have acquired wealth and do not need a thing." But you do not realize that you are wretched, pitiful, poor, blind, and naked. I counsel you to buy from me gold refined in the fire, so you can become rich; and white clothes to wear, so you can cover your shameful nakedness; and salve to put on your eyes, so you can see.
>
> Those whom I love, I rebuke and discipline. So be earnest and repent. Here I am! I stand at the door and knock. If anyone hears my voice and opens the door, I will come in and eat with that person, and they with me. (Rev 3:17-20, NIV)

The I AM, the Door to eternal life, now stands outside the doors of his own church, calling, knocking, pleading. How he longs to restore fellowship with his people! And we in the Western Church, with all its affluence and ease, hear the

same warning, pleading call. Don't lose sight of your dependence on God because you have comfort and wealth. Don't lose your effectiveness in the kingdom because you are distracted by the world's pleasures and worries. Stay focused on Jesus, humble your heart, and remember your true destiny is not in this world. Then you will enjoy the rich and joyous fellowship of Christ's presence. Then you will feast on the true food of the kingdom of heaven.

I AM

the Good Shepherd

I'm His Sheep and I Rejoice

Kindly Shepherd gentle voice
I'm his sheep and I rejoice
Tender leading, wisdom filled
Waters rushing, damned and stilled

Drinking deeply, meadow bound
Dew-fed grasses, greening ground
Sure his footing, sure his tone
Glad I follow – not alone

Kindness follows, goodness too
For his righteousness is true
Straight paths making for my feet
Danger unafraid to meet

For the table will be set
No matter what that lurking dread
Presence of my enemies
Still from fear, my heart he frees

In the valley, shadows haunt
Death and darkness hungry, gaunt
Cannot overcome or harm
For I'm carried in his arms

Patiently anointing me
Healing me he sets me free
Cup spills over, generous
His provision flows to us

Someday soon within his home
Heavenly, we'll no more roam
Until then, I'll follow on
Till life's journey path is done

Psalm 23

The LORD is my shepherd; I shall not want.

He maketh me to lie down in green pastures:
he leadeth me beside the still waters.

He restoreth my soul: he leadeth me in the paths
of righteousness for his name's sake.

Yea, though I walk through the valley of the shadow of death,
I will fear no evil: for thou art with me;
thy rod and thy staff they comfort me.

Thou preparest a table before me in the presence of mine enemies:
thou anointest my head with oil; my cup runneth over.

Surely goodness and mercy shall follow me all the days of my life:
and I will dwell in the house of the LORD for ever.

(Psalm 23:1-6, KJV)

Good Shepherd

JOHN TEN (NIV)

The sheep huddle under the brilliant glow of the strange celestial beings. The light from the dark night sky is like nothing ever seen here before. Their shepherds seem no less frightened and amazed. An unexpected pronouncement has just broken over the countryside near Bethlehem. Jesus Christ is born!

These earthy men, who spend their days in the wind, rain, and sun, hasten to follow the angel's directive. They find this wisp of a baby boy lying wrapped in a feeding manger in the sheep stable. In wonder, they take in every detail of this divine promise wrapped in human form. Then they rush out into the countryside to share the news. The Messiah is here! After so many years of waiting, the Shepherd of Israel has arrived.

For centuries sheep and shepherds have been significant and symbolic in the story of God's people. God's metaphors of shepherding his people Israel through the wilderness, Moses learning to lead those same people as a shepherd first to sheep, and the most famous of all, the Shepherd King David, a shadow of the Messiah to come.

And now he is here. The One who will stand some thirty years from now amid a hostile religious audience and declare. "*I AM the good Shepherd. The good Shepherd lays down his life for the sheep*" (Jn 10:11, NIV). Tender words in a violent age.

The Roman Empire is oppressive to the people of God, but their religious leaders enact their own form of violence. Jesus speaks to this firmly and clearly:

> *The hired hand is not the Shepherd and does not own the sheep. So when he sees the wolf coming, he abandons the sheep and runs away. Then the wolf attacks the flock and scatters it. The man runs away because he is a hired hand and cares nothing for the sheep.* (10:12-13)

He reiterates again who he is and why he's come:

> *I AM the good Shepherd; I know my sheep and my sheep know me just as the Father knows me, and I know the Father and I lay down my life for the sheep.* (10:14-15, emphasis added)

Turning to his vision of his future body, he speaks prophetically of the gospel that will soon go out around the world:

> *I have other sheep that are not of this sheep pen. I must bring them also. They, too, will listen to my voice, and there shall be one flock and one Shepherd.* (10:16)

This good Shepherd will lay down his life very soon, freely and willingly, so that all who listen to his voice may have eternal life.

> *My sheep listen to my voice; I know them, and they follow me. I give them eternal life, and they shall never perish; no one will snatch them out of my hand.* (10:27-28)

Following the Good Shepherd

"His sheep hear his voice," my dad tells me. Somehow this doesn't comfort me much when I am seventeen and struggling desperately to figure out what it means to hear the Good Shepherd's voice. I know his Holy Spirit speaks to us through his word in Scripture and through his prompting in our hearts and thoughts. But I am unsure how to sort his voice out from all the other "voices" in my world and mind.

The key to breakthrough comes slowly over months as I learn to focus on the character of my Shepherd. Gentle clarity emerges as the qualities that define his character begin to differentiate his voice from others. I begin to understand who my Shepherd is as a living person as I follow him daily through the indwelling of his Holy Spirit. Learning to know his character brings peace. Hearing him speak by his Holy Spirit brings hope and life. Following him brings rest.

Years pass. I follow him to Asia and the Middle East and back again. I pass through seasons of darkness, pain, and the valley of death; and through seasons of great clarity, hope, and vision. I see a table of provisions set over and over despite present enemies. Goodness and mercy follow me. I feel them in the beauty of my days and the promises he whispers when the storm is loudest. Through it all, he remains present with me. The one constant in all the change and chaos of uncertainty. In all the lurking dangers and triumphant victories.

I see him shepherd others, too, as they lean in and learn to listen. I catch his passion for shepherding his flock. It's all over the stories of his people as I walk in community with the global church.

I see him in the return of the lost sheep. The prodigal come home. And we rejoice together.

I see him in the green pastures of provision for the people I love, even in barren times, and I believe in his gracious kindness yet again.

I walk the valley of the shadow with loved ones. Some cross over. Some come out the other side, still journeying toward home. I see him gently tend to these beloved, his sheep. I see him carry them here, where it's darkest.

And always, in all my days and every kind of circumstance, I remember that someday I will dwell in his house forever. Our good Shepherd will lead us safely home. To follow him there is my greatest joy.

I AM

the Resurrection and the Life

A Communion – to Share in This

The silence,
It begs to be answered
Like the loud stillness after shattering glass
A thousand shards of brokenness catching light
Scattered, dangerous, like so many screaming questions

Trembling fingers clutch at what was once familiar
Only to bleed red in the grasping
What once was can never be again
Life is forever changed and time stands still

Darkness, pregnant with doubt hovers in,
Waves like so many birth pangs of fear
Wrack the mind, wring the soul of strength,
But it is all too soon, will faith be stillborn?

Like the heavy waiting before thunder
Like a storm of grief brooding, brooding
The soul waits in agony for the lightening of explanation
Static with the impact of reality

The darkness deepens and rumblings echo
Cries from some inner recess bouncing off Divine silence
The flickers and flashes of dangerous reasoning
Are an evil purple against the heavens

"My God, my God, why have you forsaken me?"
It comes echoing down the ages, the depths of all agony sounded
No soul has ever before or ever will sound such depths again.
Even heaven holds it's breath in the face of such darkness

And then the sound of rending fills the air
A curtain ripped in twain and split apart
Earth's foundations reel from the impact
And heaven rains blood.

An awesome stillness, glory burns like purifying fire
Can any question stand in such a place?
The altar of the inner holiest place flares bright as day
And suffering bows in humbled stillness, awe.

To share in this? To be and to abide?
Doubt surrenders and worship flows
To share his suffering is to also share his glory
And Faith is born again, for he has RISEN.

The Widow's Son

FIRST KINGS SEVENTEEN (NIV)

When he finds her, she is gathering sticks for a small fire. The only thing on her mind is that this is the last meal she'll cook for her and her small son. There is only a handful of flour and a little olive oil left. Then it's starvation. That's when the prophet asks her for water and food. She tells him she doesn't have anything to give.

"Don't be afraid. Just make me a little loaf of bread and then cook for you and your son. There will be enough." He promises a miracle. Miracles don't often happen during a drought in a little village like Zeraphath. But God chooses this woman and this day to reveal himself.

By faith, she shelters the prophet and feeds him. By a miracle of multiplication, the widow and her son are saved from starvation because they obey and share their bread with this stranger. It's amazing.

But then the widow's little boy gets sick. There isn't a miracle this time. He just gets worse and worse. And then he dies. "What do you have against me?" she demands of the prophet under her roof. She is grief-stricken. "Are you here to remind me of my sin and kill my son?" She feels the curse. The curse of widowhood. The curse of death. What good is a miracle if death comes anyway? She holds her son's lifeless body in her arms.

Elijah takes the boy from her. "Give him here." He takes him outside and then upstairs to his room on the roof. Laying him on the bed, he cries out to God. *"Lord my God, have you brought tragedy even on this widow I am staying with, by causing her son to die?"* (1 Kings 17:20, NIV).

He stretches his own body over the boy's body. "Give back the boy's life," he pleads. And God hears the cries of this faithful man and the grieving mother. He gives the little boy's breath of life back. He resurrects him. And the child lives.

Elijah takes him in his arms. Warm and breathing. He carries the child from his room out under the open sky and back into the house below. His mother is waiting, and when he steps in the door, Elijah announces the miracle. He bundles the boy into his mother's arms. "See, your boy is alive!"

She is flooded with joy and belief, and wonder. "Now I know that you hear from God, and what you say God says is true!" she exclaims. Her child is alive! She can hardly believe it. Yet here he is, rosy, warm, and breathing, smiling up at her. He was dead, but the God of heaven has lifted the curse of death and given him back the breath of life.

I Am the Resurrection

JOHN ELEVEN (NIV)

His friend is terribly sick. The urgent message arrives. And Jesus tarries another two days where he is. When they need him most, he hasn't come. Mary and Martha don't know what to make of this. They are devastated. Their brother dies. They wrap his body in grave clothes and put him in the tomb. Then they weep for days.

That's when Jesus decides to head in their direction. He arrives four days after the body has been put in the tomb. He knows this is for God's glory. But his friends don't. They just know he wasn't there when they needed him and aren't sure what to think.

Martha, ever practical and direct, hears Jesus is coming and goes out to meet him. "Lord, if you had showed up, my brother wouldn't have died like this. But I know God will give you what you ask for even at this late date." Her faith is strong in its desperation. She needs Jesus to be who he said he is.

Jesus reassures her that her brother will come back to life. And, of course, she assents that she believes in the final resurrection of the dead.

That's when Jesus declares his identity:

> I AM the resurrection and the life. The one who believes in me will live, even though they die; and whoever lives by believing in me will never die. Do you believe this? (Jn 11:25b-26, NIV, emphasis added)

And Martha responds with heartfelt faith even in the face of such tragedy. This dearest friend of hers is someone she knows she can trust. Even when she can't see. "*Yes, Lord, I believe that you are the Messiah, the Son of God, who is to come into the world*" (11:27).

She calls Mary to come, too. The tender sister who sits at the Lord's feet. There are few words when Mary comes to Jesus. Mostly just tears. Jesus is moved with deep compassion. He weeps with them despite knowing what is to come. He loves this family. Their pain touches him to his core.

At the grave, Jesus says, "Remove the stone."

"But Lord, the body will stink. It's been four days!" Martha protests.

Jesus pauses, "Haven't I told you that if you believe, you will see God's glory?"

They obey. The stone is rolled away, despite the stink.

Then Jesus prays. He thanks his Father for hearing him for the sake of the people witnessing this moment so they may believe he truly is the Resurrection Life. Then he shouts. "Come out, Lazarus!" And the dead man walks out of the cave into the open air, all wrapped in grave clothes.

"Unwrap those grave clothes and let him go," Jesus says.

This man was dead and is alive again! I can see the grin splitting Jesus' face as he embraces his friend. I can hear the squeals of joy as his sisters hug him in wonder.

And this foreshadows another dying and another rising. Very soon, Jesus himself will spend three days in a tomb. Then the stone will be rolled away, the power of death forever conquered as the Savior comes to life in all his glory. He is alive, for he has risen! He is the Resurrection and the Life.

Newness of Life

A half-hour past midnight, they call the midwife and her apprentices to come. This mom is powerful as she labors. The hours slip by. Her husband is half asleep with exhaustion from his work day and no sleep since, but he tries to be attentive. For those of us serving as her birth team, it is peaceful yet filled with the quiet, watchful intensity of imminent birth. We can tell this mom has done this before. It's her third child, and she labors with amazing strength, her progression unwavering.

But no matter how strong a woman is, labor is not easy. Bringing new life into the world takes everything she has. As the hours tick toward dawn, she rides the waves of pain, longing to hold her baby in her arms.

Before the sun rises, the baby's head crowns, and a boy slips into the world through a ring of fire. His cry is strong and healthy, and his mom is all smiles. He nurses heartily, his dark head cradled in her arms. Calling her own mom an hour later, she announces the arrival of new life. Her mom, who is on another continent and in another time zone, is so proud. You can hear it in her voice. "You did it! You did it!"

Her husband makes coffee and breakfast, and they insist we join them to celebrate this arrival. We are half asleep ourselves by now, but we stay to celebrate with them anyway. "Thank you so much." She says over and over. Her face is bright with joy. We assure her it was our honor to walk with her as she brought this new life into the world.

The laboring through the long night reminds me of the spiritual parallel of new birth and new life. I have watched and prayed for more than one precious prodigal. Through the years, the waves of pain have sometimes felt intolerably long and hard. But the promise of new life has been sustained. And then the morning breaks. A spiritual birth takes place, and the celebration of the return home removes all the years of sadness and waiting. The newness of life has come. And we rejoice.

How the angels rejoice over one sinner who repents! They celebrate because it reveals once again the powerful Redemption of Jesus' work of salvation and how worthy he is of such glory and honor! The magnitude of his sacrifice of love is played out life by life and all heaven stands in roaring ovation and dancing joy at his work! The Resurrection Life delights to birth new life in those who come to him. With words of welcome, he celebrates. "You were dead but are alive again! Old things have passed, and look, new things are here!"

And this is just the beginning. The ultimate resurrection is yet to come. We will dwell with God on that day in a new heaven and earth with resurrected bodies. We will celebrate an endless day of new life with Christ, that never dies.

I AM

the Way, the Truth,
and the Life

Promise of Heaven

Promise of Heaven, Jesus our Joy
Thank you for coming to show us the way
Home to the Father, life to restore
For your return, we now eagerly pray

Your kingdom coming here in our midst
Showing us Truth through God's Word as the Son
Lead us to honor all that you are
Lead us to love, make in unity One.

Show us your ways as we follow you home
Let us be faithful till faith becomes sight
Let us reflect you, our welcoming King.
Lead us to walk in eternity's light.

A Way, a Promise, a Home

EXODUS FOURTEEN (NLT)

When I read Exodus, it can seem like a simple Bible story because I've heard it all my life. But when I pause long to reflect in his presence, the story comes alive. Big and bold and filled with the impossible way through, the way to life, and the fulfilled truths of God's word to his people as he leads them toward the promised land.

A strong east wind batters the weathered face of Moses, much like the cold wind blowing in off the winter sea outside my window. I can see him in my mind's eye, standing on the bank. The glow of the pillar of cloud shines around him, though it is night. The adrenaline of the mighty deliverance is still fresh in his veins. But now, as he looks out over the dark expanse of an impassable body of water, his mind seeks Heaven's face.

Behind the newly delivered nation of slaves numbering in the thousands, the greatest army in the world closes in. It's an army he once led in battle, gathered in 600 chosen war chariots. They are intent on retaking God's people captive.

Around him, the people he has just led in deliverance cry out in terror. Didn't God promise?

> *Why did you bring us out here to die in the wilderness? Weren't there enough graves for us in Egypt? What have you done to us? Why did you make us leave Egypt? Didn't we tell you this would happen while we were still in Egypt? We said, "Leave us alone! Let us be slaves to the Egyptians. It's better to be a slave in Egypt than a corpse in the wilderness!"* (Ex. 4:11b-12 NLT)

Moses's response amid the rousing cries of fear and rumbles of impending battle is calm yet urgent:

> *Don't be afraid. Just stand still and watch the LORD rescue you today. The Egyptians you see today will never be seen again. The LORD himself will fight for you. Just stay calm.* (14:13b-14)

Ever since God called him at the burning bush he's been risking everything based on what the I AM says. Today is no different to him. He has the blueprints of heaven etched in his mind as he watches these physical events play out. The risk factors are huge. The odds are impossible. But God has spoken. And since the burning bush call he's been risking everything on that Voice.

In those moments perhaps the words of the I AM come ringing back:

> *Order the Israelites to turn back and camp by Pi-hahiroth between Migdol and the sea. Camp there along the shore, across from Baal-zephon. Then Pharaoh will think, 'The Israelites are confused. They are trapped in the wilderness!' And once again I will harden*

Pharaoh's heart, and he will chase after you. I have planned this in order to display my glory through Pharaoh and his whole army. After this the Egyptians will know that I AM the Lord! *(14:2-4a)*

Even as the people cry out the Lord speaks again to Moses:

Why are you crying out to me? Tell the people to get moving! Pick up your staff and raise your hand over the sea. Divide the water so the Israelites can walk through the middle of the sea on dry ground. And I will harden the hearts of the Egyptians, and they will charge in after the Israelites. My great glory will be displayed through Pharaoh and his troops, his chariots, and his charioteers. When my glory is displayed through them, all Egypt will see my glory and know that I AM the Lord! *(14:15-18)*

Moses moves to obey God, and the angel that has been guiding them forward moves to the margin of space between the army and the Israelite encampment. God does not speak without empowering. He has provided a rear guard. A wall of fire will separate the two groups as Moses stretches out his rod over the waters in front of them.

Darkness falls. A strong east wind blows in, troubling the waters into walls on either side of a path of dry ground. The Israelites see the miracle and move to obey the word of God. Take the risk and walk into the sea bed. The only way is through. God will lead them through the sea, and God will get glory through the Egyptian army.

The Egyptians pursue. Maybe the hearts of the people feel fresh terror as they hurry through the sea path. These enemies are not easily deterred. Is God's rescue plan going to work?

But just before dawn, when the hour seems darkest, God moves in for the next phase of his plan. He strikes with confusion. Twisted chariot wheels. "Let's get out of here!" The terrified warriors yell. Horses scream. Chariots mire and lose their wheels. The warriors can tell God is fighting for his people.

As the sun rises, God and Moses partner in completing the victory plan. All the Israelites are safely on shore now.

Raise your hand over the sea again. Then the waters will rush back and cover the Egyptians and their chariots and charioteers. (14:26b)

Moses obeys. The mighty walls of water rush back into place. Not a single Egyptian warrior escapes. God's rescue plan is complete. When the people see the mighty power that the LORD has unleashed against the Egyptians, they are filled with awe before him. They put their faith in the LORD and in his servant Moses. The risk of hearing from God proved worth it. But the risks will continue. It's what a life of faith entails.

As I AM leads his people through the wilderness to a place of covenant and beyond, they will face many more impossibilities. They must follow the pillar of fire and cloud, as God himself shows them the way. They must lean into the truth of his word repeatedly as he speaks to them. Their lives depend on him to protect, provide, and fulfill all he has said until they flourish in the land he will give them. He is their salvation in the Red Sea and their way through the wilderness. His words are the truth that sets them free; his provision of a new way of life after slavery is their way to flourishing, and the place he provides them is an invitation home.

I Am the Way Home

JOHN FOURTEEN (NIV)

"Do not let your hearts be troubled. You believe in God; believe also in me. My Father's house has many rooms; if that were not so, would I have told you that I am going there to prepare a place for you? And if I go and prepare a place for you, I will come back and take you to be with me that you also may be where I am. You know the way to the place where I am going."

Thomas said to him, "Lord, we don't know where you are going, so how can we know the way?"

Jesus answered, "I AM the way and the truth and the life. No one comes to the Father except through me. If you really know me, you will know my Father as well. From now on, you do know him and have seen him."

Philip said, "Lord, show us the Father and that will be enough for us."

Jesus answered: "Don't you know me, Philip, even after I have been among you such a long time? Anyone who has seen me has seen the Father. How can you say, 'Show us the Father'? Don't you believe that I am in the Father, and that the Father is in me? The words I say to you I do not speak on my own authority. Rather, it is the Father, living in me, who is doing his work. Believe me when I say that I am in the Father and the Father is in me; or at least believe on the evidence of the works themselves. Very truly I tell you, whoever believes in me will do the works I have been doing, and they will do even greater things than these, because I am going to the Father. And I will do whatever you ask in my name, so that the Father may be glorified in the Son. You may ask me for anything in my name, and I will do it.

"If you love me, keep my commands. And I will ask the Father, and he will give you another advocate to help you and be with you forever— the Spirit of truth. The world cannot accept him, because it neither sees him nor knows him. But you know him, for he lives with you and will be in you. I will not leave you as orphans; I will come to you. Before long, the world will not see me anymore, but you will see me. Because I live, you also will live. On that day you will realize that I am in my Father, and you are in me, and I am in you. Whoever has my commands and keeps them is the one who loves me. The one who loves me will be loved by my Father, and I too will love them and show myself to them."

Then Judas (not Judas Iscariot) said, "But, Lord, why do you intend to show yourself to us and not to the world?"

Jesus replied, "Anyone who loves me will obey my teaching. My Father will love them, and we will come to them and make our home with them. Anyone who does not love me will not obey my teaching. These words you hear are not my own; they belong to the Father who sent me.

"All this I have spoken while still with you. But the Advocate, the Holy Spirit, whom the Father will send in my name, will teach you all things and will remind you of everything I have said to you. Peace I leave with you; my peace I give you. I do not give to you as the world gives. Do not let your hearts be troubled and do not be afraid.

"You heard me say, 'I am going away and I am coming back to you.' If you loved me, you would be glad that I am going to the Father, for the Father is greater than I. I have told you now before it happens, so that when it does happen you will believe. I will not say much more to you, for the prince of this world is coming. He has no hold over me, but he comes so that the world may learn that I love the Father and do exactly what my Father has commanded me."
(John 14:1-31, NIV)

People of Welcome

"Why did we take that path?" My mom asked with the clarity of hindsight.

"We didn't know the right way yet, I guess," I shrugged. "You don't know what you don't know, and when you don't know the way by experience, it's easy to get lost."

That morning, we'd set off into the dunes with the goal of reaching the ocean. We'd been warned to mark our path back off the beach, as every path leading from the beach to the dunes was very much the same, but no one had mentioned how hard it might be to discern which path led to the beach initially. So, following a pair of footprints in sand wet from the previous day's rain (presumably a man with his dog from the size of the boot tracks), we set off to arrive breathless on a dead-end sand cliff that led into valleys of thickets and more rolling dunes, with no path through to the ocean, rolling just within sight on the horizon, half a mile away. After several attempts at backtracking, we eventually found our path through and made it to the beach.

As we wandered feeling helpless in those dunes along the rugged, wild coast, I had to think of many of my displaced friends' journeys. As they flee violence at home, they make their way through unknown and often dangerous territory, searching for a way to life. On that journey, they ache for safety, welcome, and home. I have served in places foreign to both me and my displaced friends, seeking to ease their journey along the way. In those places, they have often welcomed me as much as I have welcomed them. And in that shared welcome, my friends and I often found ourselves a little closer to the sense of place and belonging we were made for. A little closer to a sense of home.

I thought of our Hispanic taxi driver, once an immigrant himself, who had welcomed us the night before with unsolicited generosity and wise suggestions about safety in the area where we were staying. There was nothing in it for him; it was simply an extension of his identity. The concern was as touching as it was genuine, and I wondered how much his memories of the vulnerability of arrival had shaped the welcoming person he had become.

As the body of Christ, we are called to be people of welcome. We are called to be people who reflect the way home. We have been welcomed into the kingdom of light and love, and as followers of Jesus, we are called to embody and reflect Jesus in the world in the same way. As we open our lives and homes to receiving the stranger, caring for the vulnerable, and speaking for the marginalized, a world filled with confusion and fear can become a place where people are welcomed into hope and healing. As we love our neighbors, the kingdom of heaven among us becomes a place of belonging where there is nourishment for everyone around the table.

When Thomas asked Jesus how they could know the way to where he was going, Jesus reassured him that he was the way home, the Truth to orient by, and the Life everlasting. As people of Jesus, we, the Church, are called to welcome those all around us to join us in following the Way, Truth, and Life as a person - Jesus, the way to God, and the Way home to where we belong.

I AM

the True Vine

The voice at cool of day calls, "Come and listen,
Come walk and talk with me; your heart's desired
Come glory crowned, my image-bearing lover
Come find your rest from toil that makes you tired

Abide in me; this vineyard home, our treasure
The wine grapes grown on vines he's grafted in
The Master Gardener, whose care and wisdom, tender
Prunes for your good, the things that lead to sin

Stay; let the lifeblood of my vine sustain you.
Branches that bear the fruit of kingdom good
Let not your hearts be troubled; this I tell you
So that in me, your trials can be withstood

Have peace, your wholeness born of finding shelter
Abide in me, flourishing in life as Mine
This sacred living in the vine, belonging
Gives heartening grace, empowering fruit divine"

Master Gardener

GENESIS ONE THROUGH THREE

Life with God began in a garden. As the hospitable Master Gardener, that first Eden was designed as a place to nourish a life filled with beauty, flourishing, and participation. In its cool evenings, Adam and Eve walked and talked with God. During the perfect, sunny days, they tended to the plants and animals and enjoyed abundant fruit and food grown there. Stretching their limits, they no doubt made new daily discoveries as they learned to tend to the land God had entrusted them to steward with him.

I imagine that Eden was like the beauty I've witnessed in the country of Costa Rica, known as one of the greenest and happiest countries in the world. When I visit, I am perpetually awed by the variety of the rich blue and green landscape, clear, crisp skies, lush forests, and a stunning diversity of flora and fauna. Colorful flowering plants and shrubs bloom everywhere, brilliant birds flash their colors, brooks sing and gurgle their way over shallow rocky beds, and birdsong fills the air in symphony from morning to night. In Eden, dew fell to water the vegetation morning and evening, and its natural beauty was perfect.

But far greater in importance to the Master Gardener, than all of this beauty was the relational freedom shared between God and man. The sting of the curse was not yet felt, and shame had not yet inhibited or clouded the beauty of God's plan and design for humankind. This was most keenly displayed not in the perfection of beauty in the landscape but in the intimate knowing of God and man as they worked and fellowshipped heart to heart.

In an echo of Eden in all of us, people are still drawn to gardens today — from the famed UNESCO World Heritage Site, Vallée de Mai on the island of Praslin with its Edenic Myths, to the seven airport gardens in Seoul's Incheon International Airport, including the famous star garden with around 150 species of plants for travelers to enjoy on their way around the globe. Hubs of communal life and personal rejuvenation, temple gardens, city parks, backyard sanctuaries, and farmhouse vegetable gardens are all places designed and maintained to provide some hospitable feast, whether of beauty for the soul, quiet for the mind, or healthy food to eat.

And behind the architecture and careful garden design is always the gardener. That hospitable creative who foresaw that this living, breathing, vibrant space would become a sanctuary for other image bearers who hunger and thirst for beauty and rest in their souls. That invitation to create a place for flourishing resounds with the character of God. All beauty is an invitation back to his glory. All design reflected, even poorly, is imprinted with his loving and attentive desire to dwell with man in relational goodness and life-giving shalom.

You Are My Friends!

JOHN FIFTEEN (NLT)

The lamp wicks flicker in their olive oil, the broken flatbread fragments scattered lightly across the low table. This is the bread he has broken as a declaration of salvation. Their wine stands in earthen cups as faces are turned earnestly on the Rabbi. This is the wine he has used to declare that his blood will usher in the New Covenant.

He continuously surprises them—his washing of their feet and announcement of a betrayer among them has already upset the typical Passover supper traditions. He talks about peace and trials and how he will send a Helper to teach them—this Comforter as the Holy Spirit will lead them into all truth and remind them of what he has said.

Now, using language familiar to all Israelites, of vineyards and fruit, as metaphors of Israel's historic unfaithfulness to God, of the promised land, of judgment, and righteousness and redemption, Jesus speaks earnestly and tenderly:

I AM the true grapevine, and my Father is the gardener. He cuts off every branch of mine that doesn't produce fruit, and he prunes the branches that do bear fruit so they will produce even more. You have already been pruned and purified by the message I have given you.

Remain in me, and I will remain in you. For a branch cannot produce fruit if it is severed from the vine, and you cannot be fruitful unless you remain in me. Yes, I AM the vine; you are the branches. Those who remain in me, and I in them, will produce much fruit. For apart from me you can do nothing.

Anyone who does not remain in me is thrown away like a useless branch and withers. Such branches are gathered into a pile to be burned. But if you remain in me and my words remain in you, you may ask for anything you want, and it will be granted!

When you produce much fruit, you are my true disciples. This brings great glory to my Father. I have loved you even as the Father has loved me. Remain in my love. When you obey my commandments, you remain in my love, just as I obey my Father's commandments and remain in his love. I have told you these things so that you will be filled with my joy. Yes, your joy will overflow!

This is my commandment: Love each other in the same way I have loved you. There is no greater love than to lay down one's life for one's friends. You are my friends if you do what I command. I no longer call you slaves, because a master doesn't confide in his slaves. Now you are my friends, since I have told you everything the Father told me. You didn't choose me. I chose you. I appointed you to go and produce lasting fruit, so that the Father will give you whatever you ask for, using my name. This is my command: Love each other. (John 15:1-17, NLT)

Nurturing Disciplines

EXODUS FOURTEEN (NLT)

It is a cold November night, and we've lit the candles to combat the sense of dullness and chill outside. My friend and I sit in easy companionship, discussing the journey of discipleship to Jesus and what it means to belong in the kingdom of heaven.

The conversation naturally turns to relationships with God and with others. "How do you combat performance without going into isolation or distancing in relationship to God and others?" she asks. "How do you cultivate spiritual disciplines and healthy use of authority and influence, flowing out of love and honesty and not hard work or independence?"

"How do you feel about our friendship and the conversation we are having right now?" I ask.

"It's an easy joy," she responds with a smile. "I feel the same about my conversations with God in contemplative prayer. But I don't think of that as a discipline. I think of discipline as going to the gym to get stronger, not something I find easy and enjoyable."

"What if spiritual disciplines are something that nurtures your relationship with God and cultivates spiritual maturity?" I wonder aloud. "What if the way you enjoy authentic conversations with God and other believers is actually the spiritual discipline God is inviting you to in this season of your life to produce the fruit of intimacy?"

"I like that idea," she muses. "And it comes back to remembering my place in the kingdom. I want to bring him glory and fulfill my calling, and I feel called to be a light to the world around me. But my significance comes through my identity as the beloved, and my calling flows out of that, not vice versa. I don't have to work my way into my calling. He calls me, and I can only fully bring God glory when I live out of that love by accepting it as true."

"How does that realization impact how you feel about your relationship with God and his invitation to being called and practicing spiritual disciplines?" I ask.

"It's powerful," she says thoughtfully. "It stills me. Leaves me in awe." She pauses, then adds. "And it makes me feel very secure."

As I ponder my friend's words, I realize she summarizes really well what it means to live abiding in Jesus. In finding our heart's home in him and receiving our identity with him, we can live in his kingdom every day. When we live in this heart posture, and our habits and decisions flow out of that, our spiritual formation leads to relationships based on love and not performance. The desired outcome is communities of interdependence that produce the fruit of unity and bring God glory, pointing to a day very soon when we will all be home, perfected in loving relationship with Christ and one another, forever.

I Am Coming Soon!

REVELATIONS TWENTY-TWO (NIV)

Then the angel showed me a river of the water of life, as clear as crystal, flowing from the throne of God and of the Lamb down the middle of the main street of the city. On either side of the river stood a tree of life, bearing twelve kinds of fruit and yielding a fresh crop for each month. And the leaves of the tree are for the healing of the nations.

No longer will there be any curse. The throne of God and of the Lamb will be within the city, and his servants will worship him. They will see his face, and his name will be on their foreheads. There will be no more night in the city, and they will have no need for the light of a lamp or of the sun. For the Lord God will shine on them, and they will reign forever and ever.

Then the angel said to me, "These words are faithful and true. The Lord, the God of the spirits of the prophets, has sent his angel to show his servants what must soon take place."

"Behold, I AM coming soon. Blessed is the one who keeps the words of prophecy in this book. (Revelations 22:1-7, NIV; emphasis added)

Behold, I am coming soon, and my reward is with me, to give to each one according to what he has done. I AM the Alpha and the Omega, the First and the Last, the Beginning and the End."

Blessed are those who wash their robes, so that they may have the right to the tree of life and may enter the city by its gates. But outside are the dogs, the sorcerers, the sexually immoral, the murderers, the idolaters, and everyone who loves and practices falsehood.

"I, Jesus, have sent my angel to give you this testimony for the churches. I AM the Root and the Offspring of David, the bright Morning Star."

The Spirit and the bride say, "Come!" Let the one who hears say, "Come!" And let the one who is thirsty come, and the one who desires the water of life drink freely. (22:12-17, emphasis added)

He who testifies to these things says, **"Yes, I AM coming soon."** Amen. Come, Lord Jesus!

The grace of the Lord Jesus be with all the saints. (22:20-21, emphasis added)

Amen.

Acknowledgments

AUTHOR: Creating this book was another collaborative journey filled with goodness. I'm incredibly grateful to continue to create with such skilled and gracious artists!

Thank you, Mom, for the memories made despite detours, canceled accommodations, and an ice storm that started our book-writing and art retreat off with some wild memories. The hours and days that unfolded in an unexpected but beautiful mountaintop destination were truly memorable and filled with peace and pleasure. Thank you for seeing life and goodness in my words and envisioning God's heart and message in your incredible paintings that complement the text for this book so well. I love partnering with you to create beauty for his glory!

Thank you, Tracia, for once again tuning in with your skill and masterful attention to detail to take an unfinished work and polish it to completion. You make our team complete, and it's always such a joy to work with you!

Thank you to Delight, Bri, and Annie, valued friends who gave wise and gracious feedback during editing. I'm better because of you, and this book is better because of your thoughtful input.

ARTIST: Thank you, Rachael, for welcoming me to join you in another book project. It blessed me to watch you seek God for clear direction in what to write about and how the book should unfold during our retreat, and I love the pattern he gave you for exploring each name of I AM. Once again, I felt we were working together with him for his glory. Our writing/painting trips are filled with worship and joy! Later, when I painted from home to finish the illustrations for this book, you blessed me with words of encouragement, celebrating each painting with me. Your insightful writing inspires me!

I'm blessed by my children and grandchildren, who fill my life with sunshine. I appreciate your kind, encouraging words about my art and your love and fellowship on our earthly pilgrimage. Through you, I have seen more of our incomparable God.

Thank you, Tracia, for taking my artwork, digitizing it, and laying it out beautifully! Without you, there would be no finished book.

Most of all, thank you to you, "I AM"! You have graciously made yourself known to us in word pictures we can understand and relate to; you who ARE and have always been, who shepherds, feeds, and leads us with such love and wisdom, are amazing beyond explanation. My Redeemer, my Light, I rejoice in you!!

Artist Biographies

Rachael Lofgren

AUTHOR:

As a communicator and storyteller, Rachael seeks to see God's bigger story woven through people's everyday lives. The author of numerous published biographical and historical works with a background in communications and international humanitarian aid, her passion is to champion personal discipleship, healing, community, and maturity in the body of Christ among the nations. Nourishing others in their relationship with Christ and their understanding of his love brings her joy.

Tracia Ropp

GRAPHIC DESIGNER:

Tracia's love for typography, layout, and all things InDesign is fueled by a passion for the Creator and the way he creates. She loves the synergy that happens when individuals come together to collaborate as agents of goodness, beauty, and light that pushes back darkness.

Patti Lofgren

ARTIST:

As an artist, Patti enjoys working in various mediums, including watercolor and oil paint. Passionate about art and education for the glory of God, along with homeschooling, she enjoys sharing art experiences with her children and grandchildren. She sees the beauty in the world as God's canvas of love, and for her, art is both a form of communal pleasure and of worship.

This artistic mother-daughter duo delights in working together to produce material that inspires others to understand God's love personally and worship him more fully through their combination of art and words.

Artist Contact:

EMAIL:

singingsparrowpress@gmail.com

WEBSITE:

www.singingsparrowpress.com